# A TASTE OF

# LIFE AND LOVE

# IN

# DARKEST PERU

*Very Best Wishes for now and the future*

## Bronwen Grono

*Bronwen Grono*

ISBN-13: 978-1515058526

ISBN-10:  1515058522

## Acknowledgements

I must thank above all the amazing Suzan Collins, without whom I would not have managed to do this.

I also thank Jo Wilde for producing the book you hold in your hand.

I would like to thank Mark Smith and Gina and Richard of the Coconut Loft in Lowestoft for their critique.

And finally, my friends Millie, Iris and Linda, and my son Carlos and his girlfriend Monica for their encouragement.

# CONTENTS

## THE HAT

To return to Peru I decided to get a new wardrobe and I wanted something really special to travel in. So my sister and I went off to Swansea, one of the nearest big towns, for a day out shopping.

I wanted to look elegant but I needed to be comfortable as well. Inside British Home Stores we started checking out the dresses.

"What colour are you looking for, Sis?" Sue asked me.

"No special colour, but something bright and summery," I answered.

She came over to me holding up a linen dress in a lovely shade of melon. Since I'd lost some weight I thought I might be able to wear it.

"Accessories?" she asked.

We found some brown shoes, a brown handbag, and a silky brown picture hat. I loved wearing hats!

After the long flight, I arrived in Lima airport and got off the plane still wearing my lovely hat. I had convinced myself that since my hair was a mess I needed to keep it on.

I was a sensation! People didn't wear hats in the coastal region of Peru and heads turned to look at me as I made my way through the crowds. I felt like a film star!

"You look stunning!" Carlos murmured after holding me at arm's length to look at me.

Shortly afterwards we boarded a flight to Tacna to fly south.

Once there, we took a taxi to the Tourist Hotel where we would stay for a few days before travelling up to Toquepala, the copper mine, which was two hours' journey away by road.

Before going into the dining room I checked my hair and decided not to take my hat off. Secretly, I liked all the attention I was getting from wearing it.

The only people who wear hats in Peru are the Indian peoples in the Andean region. They have a different type of hat for each region.

A year later we returned to the Tourist Hotel on a weekend away.

As we sat in the dining room one of the waiters said to me

"Senora, how nice to see you again!"

"Thank you," I said "I can see you remember me!"

"Of course," he replied, "You're the lady in the hat!"

## SOLITUDE

Looking out on the grey, grey dawn

my soul shivered and knew that

it was one with this new morn.

All that I had lived was useless now.

Memories crowd and pierce

the blanket covering my heart.

Excruciating hurt!

How will I ever live with it?

Day after day there is an all enfolding

nothing inside of me.

When will my heart stop grieving?

I had three little souls in my charge.

Delicate things like unfolding flowers,

like pearls without price.

Where are those precious beings now?

Are they lost?

They're far away and that's why

my soul feels this terrible iciness.

I've lost those beings which gave me warmth.

Oh! How my heart longs for that warmth once again

so that it might uncurl,

and their laughter could enter in

like the pale golden glow of sunshine on a winter's day.

In a crowded room filled with happiness,

and ordinary people who know how to love,

now laughing, now crying

but together in their lovely ordinary lives,

I feel the loneliness surrounding me

like being enveloped in the quiet

of a deep cold lake.

The sounds of these warm humans

hardly reach my consciousness.

How very lonely I am!

How I wish for those other years

when I too, was just an ordinary person

like those around me.

Lucky people! I yearn to join your laughter

and be like you.

But my soul has been damned to Hell!

## LOVE - AGAIN

Love again, bringing me new life,

the awakening of a new dawn,

the same old feelings rife

in my heart and body drawn

ever outwards with each loving caress.


How lonely I was until you came,

with your beautiful stirring touch.

Different! But inevitably the same!

The same old story that I love so much.

You - a Greek god in modern dress.

I want you now in the dead of the night

holding me close 'til we become one

and our spirits soar together out of sight

to heights unreached before by any man.


Out into the velvet starriness of the sky,

far away on wings we're flying.

And then - a resettling - hearts still,

and the slow ebb tide of our passion dying.


I'm with you, my darling

wherever you will.

Cleave to me, cling to me,

I am your own.

HIS SON

This child of mine

so dear,

strong and beautiful and fine.

The living memory

of another.


His warmth next to me,

so near

enveloping me in tenderness

and awakening

my love.


A love transferred

from father to son.

The future promise

of him becoming one with

all that he was.


An ever living memory

of love, though gone

which lives on still

in his son.

SINCHI

My son Carlos' father died when he was just two and a half years old.

He had vague memories of him coming back from his morning run and then swinging him up onto his broad shoulders for a short trek to the bakery to get his favourite baguette for breakfast.

One day after he'd been rummaging in a closet he'd found a music tape with a special chant on it:

"I want to be a Sinchi

A town to rescue

From pain and desperation

Opening the doors of the sky

To parachute in

Like an angel

From God.


To dry the tears of a town

Devastated by

So large an earthquake.

It erased my beautiful Huaylas

From the map.

The gigantic apu  Huascaran

Swallowed Yungay in seconds.

Brave  Sinchis , emissaries

Who gave us back hope

Falling from the firmament

To console the survivors

And bury the dead.

Sinchis, green angels,

Sent by God

In answer to

The prayers of the people

Strong brave Sinchis of the 70s"

Carlos asked me "What's a Sinchi?"

It was a very special part of the recent history of Peru. How could I explain it to a 6 year old? I tried to make it clear.

"It is a very special group of men in the Police Force. It's called an elite force. Your dad was a founder member. He was one of the men trained by another special group called The Green Berets of the United States. Then he and the others in the group started a sort of camp which was a Sinchi Base in Mazamari in the jungle."

"What did they do?" He asked.

"Well, there were some bad men who were terrorists and they had their own camps in the jungle and your father and his men had to fight them."

I couldn't give him all the gory details. These brave men were dropped into the jungle by parachute and then they crept up to the subversives and slit their throats. They couldn't use guns as that would draw the attention of other terrorist cells nearby.

So I said, "Well, they had to defend themselves, you know, and some men always die in wars and so it was very dangerous."

"My dad must have been very brave!"

His father was well known in the force for many acts of bravery. He had almost died once in an uprising by the terrorists on a sugar plantation in the north of Peru after being ambushed. His instincts told him which escape route to take and that saved him.

After he died in a car accident in 1977, a graduating class of Sinchis in Mazamari was named after him.

The terrorists were connected to drug traffickers which gave them the economic resources to acquire the guns and equipment needed to wage their war. They called themselves 'Sendero Luminoso' - The Shining Path.

When the Senderistas were eventually defeated after the capture of their leader, a philosopher called Abimael Guzman, in 1994, the elite group of Sinchis stayed on in the jungle to confront the drug traffickers.

They fight on in Huallaga, Maranon, Tambopata and Urubamba where the heat is intolerable and temperatures reach 40°c. They stay in camps with no electricity nor running water. They spend all their waking hours repressing the production of cocaine, eradicating laboratories and destroying dozens of illegal airports.

To date they have destroyed organizations called the Mosquitos, Crystal and Uncle Abraham amongst others.

The Sinchis have earned their part in the history of Peru.

# A  HOUSE IN THE DESERT

A house

In the  desert !

A woman

Waiting for  me !

Love , passion

And tenderness

For me

Under the sky of blue

The hot sun,

On the

Wave – specked beaches

She waits for me

Only me.

And I will

Come to her

Under the blue sky

The hot sun

And on the wave – specked

Beaches.

And I will

Love her there

Until

We become

One.

## MY PART TIME LOVE

He's mine

Occasionally

Unfortunately

He's mine

Only once in a while.


How I wish

He were mine

For always

For ever and a day.

How I wish

We could live

Together

And never be away

From each other.

My part-time love

Where are you

Tonight?

Whose arms

Are around you

Holding you

Tight?

Come see me

Soon

And not in three months' time

'Cause part-time lovin'

Is really a crime.

I need you full time

Not part-time you see

Say you'll think it over

Say you'll think of me

Not only

As your part-time love.

## THE IMPORTANCE OF BEING CARLOS.

"My name's Carlos. What's yours?" The dark handsome man said. He was sitting on the stone steps of the staircase in the hall of the Sorbonne in Paris.

"Where are you from?" I asked. "Peru," he said in a sultry voice which sent a shiver down my spine. This Peruvian god was actually smiling at me.

We left the university together. Later, after his kisses made me reel, he murmured, "I'd like to take you to Peru and lock you up in a tower and keep you only for me." Jealous, I thought. And how right that proved to be!

"This is Captain Carlos Ronceros," my friend said as I got out of the pool to join them. "We're going to my place for lunch. Care to come? I jumped into the captain's truck and off we went to the barbecue.

Another friend was waiting for Jane at her place and I was left in the garden with the handsome captain. He leaned towards me and kissed me on the cheek. "I'd like to see you afterwards," he whispered. And so started the romance with the great love of my life, which only ended when he died in a car accident at the age of forty.

"Would you like to come to my place for a drink, Carlos?"

"Really?" asked the tall young man with huge liquid brown eyes. I'd been very lonely for a year since my brave captain had died. And his name was Carlos, too, wasn't it? The torrid romance ended some months later. Older women and younger men rarely works out!

"Hello, remember me?" Asked a voice from the car pulling up beside me. I bent down to look in at the lovely smile of the man at the wheel.

"Yes, you're the lawyer who was one of my students at the Language Centre last term."

"That's right! Would you like a ride somewhere?"

"No I'm just going to work at the Centre around the corner"

"Well, how about a date then?"

"I'd like that. Can I call you later?"

"I'll look forward to that. Here's my card!"

"Interesting", I thought while I popped it into my bag. What was his name? I fished the card out again. Carlos, of course!

"Yes, I'd really like to get married again!" The man was from Trujillo. He was the sign of Aries – quite compatible with my sign of Saggitarius and - most important of all - his name was Carlos!

Two days later he appeared at my door in Chaclacayo, and he popped the question that very night. So, I was getting married again!

It lasted just over a year while I was in Wales visiting my mother and he was in Peru taking care of his sick mother.

Upon returning I looked at him and I knew it was another mistake!

## AFTER THE SUMMER

The summer of my love

Is over.

I can feel the chills

Of autumn

Deep inside me

I feel so lonely!

His love,

Which warmed me,

Has gone.

I feel such a longing for him

His arms around me

His kisses

And caresses

I miss the love that has gone

After the summer.

After the summer

The chill winds

Of autumn come

Leaving my soul empty

Bereft of the warmth

Of the sun

That he brought me

And warmed me,

Body and soul,

Filling me with

The golden happiness

That has now gone

With the last day of summer

## SUMMER RAIN

It's raining.

I'd like to walk with you now.

It's so fresh.

Summer rain wetting my brow.


We could walk together,

Hand in hand

Our faces wet

Hand in hand

Cool and fresh.

How beautiful the rain is!

The night is so cool

And I'm thinking about you

So I'm not really alone.

It's a good feeling

To know you're not so alone.


The rain's on my face

And all over me,

Wetting my hair,

Refreshing me.

And I'm not really alone

With the rain

Because you,

You are inside me

We are one – we two.

## THE MAGIC HOUR

The magic hour!

When the troubles

Of the day

Are over

And the velvet dark

Descends upon

The earth.

A hush overcomes

The meadows

And the birds a fluttering

Settle on their nests

Welcoming

The cool quiet night

A night of dreams

When weary limbs unfold

In repose

And wrinkled brows

Are smoothed

From all their

Woes

And we escape

To join the cosmos

From whence

We come

To renew our strength

And continue

Life's battle

In the way

God planned.

## CHRISTMAS IN PERU

"It's looking like Christmas, Mum!"

I looked up from decorating my tree with big white bows, as my son came into the front patio of the house.

His tanned body glistened and his sun – bleached hair hung wet to his shoulders. He carried his surf board under his arm and Richel, his friend, came in with him. They padded over the tiles in their bare feet and stopped under the white arched colonnade to admire the six foot tree.

"Blanco con dorado," said Richel. "White and gold! Shouldn't it be red and gold?"

"I've had white and gold for the last few Christmases and I like it better," I replied.

It was December 24th - Christmas Eve. After finishing the tree I put up the Nacimiento or Nativity Scene as is the custom in Peru, a Catholic country.

There was a knock on the door and my neighbour, Rita, came in.

"They've taken the Virgin from the grotto down to the church ready for the procession this evening. Are you coming with us later?

"Yes, I'll come a little way towards the end," I told her.

The grotto was in a small park in front of my house. 'La Virgen de las Mercedes' stood in a glass urn at the entrance to the park. In front of her there were benches for people to sit and recite the rosary. I would catch up with the procession around the little seaside town of San Bartolo later on in the evening.

Next on my list of things to do was the turkey, and so I went into the kitchen to prepare it and pop it into the oven. Even though I'd lived in Peru for so long, I still made a Christmas lunch similar to that back home in Britain. There were no sprouts or parsnips here, so we had beans and carrots, roast potatoes and gravy. The big difference was that we ate lunch on the 24th and not on the 25th.

"That was delicious, mum," said Carlos. "I'll help you clear the table."

"Would you like some panettone now?" I asked him.

"No, I'll have some at midnight, with the hot chocolate you're going to make."

And then he was off to the beach again where he would surf until sunset.

It was very hot at 4pm and so I lay down in my white-walled bedroom for a siesta. At 5.30 I got up to take a shower.

As I dressed, Rita came in again and we sat and talked for a while.

"Come and sit out here by the tree. I've got a few more presents to wrap."

"It's a lovely tree. I love to see it in the evening when it's all lit up," she said.

It was the last thing my late husband had bought me just before he died. He'd known how much I loved the Christmas celebration with a tree. Poor people in Peru could not afford to have one.

At 10 that evening, Rita and I made our way to where the procession was slowly moving along the promenade and back up to the grotto. The large statue was carried on a wooden stretcher by six of the faithful, and people jostled on all sides to touch the base and ask for Her blessing.

We shuffled along behind with our flowers to place at her feet.

And then She was back in her urn in the grotto, where a basket had been placed in readiness for the Christ child on the stroke of midnight.

And the people prayed:

"Santa Maria,

Mother of God, pray for us sinners now and at the hour of our death

Amen."

I could see Carlos going into the house from the corner of my eye, so I moved to give my neighbours a hug as things drew to a close.

"Feliz Navidad! Happy Christmas!"

It was a quarter to twelve and my son and I stood by the tree with a bottle of champagne as we waited for the clock to strike.

"Feliz Navidad, Mama!" Carlos laughed, hugging me.

The coffee table was laid out with the hot spiced chocolate and panettone which we had after our champagne. Then Carlos was off to light fireworks with his friends outside.

"See you later, mum."

The next day, the 25th of December, our friends began arriving from Lima, the capital, as it was customary to go to the beach on this day of the festivities. They came laden with presents, panettone, and salads, along with chicken and chorizos for the barbecue later.

There were about ten of us as we walked the short distance to the sea.

"Here let me carry that parasol," Jaime said.

"Ok, I'll carry my chair," I replied.

The sun was already scorching and everyone had spread on a liberal coating of sun-tan lotion.

We lay on the beach laughing and talking and going in and out of the sea to cool off.

At about 2pm, I said

"Well, I'm off back to the house to light the barbecue ready for when you all come back up."

"I'll do that, Mum," said Carlos, who had given up his morning of surfing to spend time with the visitors.

Later on the happy sun-tanned group came in for the barbecue and to listen to the carols on the stereo.

Carlos said to me "Que linda la Navidad!   How beautiful Christmas is!!"

## About the author

Bronwen Grono met and married a Peruvian while studying in Paris.

Consequently she lived in Peru for forty years, during which she taught English in the university and in a British International school.

She returned to the UK after having cancer, to join her son who had returned here to work.

11683038R00034

Printed in Great Britain
by Amazon.co.uk, Ltd.,
Marston Gate.